# Laura Ingalls Wilder

### By Wil Mara

**Consultant**
Jeanne Clidas, Ph.D.
National Reading Consultant
and
Professor of Reading, SUNY Brockport

Children's Press ®
A Division of Scholastic Inc.
New York   Toronto   London   Auckland   Sydney
Mexico City   New Delhi   Hong Kong
Danbury, Connecticut

Designer: Herman Adler Design
Photo Researcher: Caroline Anderson
The photo on the cover shows Laura Ingalls Wilder at age seventeen.

**Library of Congress Cataloging-in-Publication Data**

Mara, Wil.
  Laura Ingalls Wilder / by Wil Mara.
    p. cm. — (Rookie biographies)
Includes index.
Summary: Presents a brief look at the life of Laura Ingalls Wilder,
famed author of the "Little House" books.
  ISBN 0-516-22855-2 (lib. bdg.)    0-516-27840-1 (pbk.)
  1. Wilder, Laura Ingalls, 1867-1957—Juvenile literature. 2. Authors,
American—20th century—Biography—Juvenile literature. 3. Frontier and
pioneer life—United States—Juvenile literature. 4. Children's
stories—Authorship—Juvenile literature. [1. Wilder, Laura Ingalls,
1867-1957. 2. Authors, American. 3. Women—Biography.] I. Title. II.
Series: Rookie biography.
  PS3545.I342 Z7625 2003
  813'.52—dc21
                              2002015156

Can you imagine life without
telephones, televisions, or movies?

Laura Ingalls lived this way for many years. She was born in Wisconsin on February 7, 1867.

Her family lived on a farm.

Running a farm was hard work. If you needed food, you had to grow it yourself. If it was cold, you had to build a fire.

8

Laura helped run the family farm. She had three sisters who also helped. Their names were Mary, Carrie, and Grace.

Laura and her family moved a lot. Her father was always looking for a place where the family could have a better life.

They went to Missouri, Kansas, Iowa, Minnesota, and South Dakota.

CANADA

North
West ✦ East
South

MONTANA

NORTH
DAKOTA

MINNESOTA

MICHIGAN

SOUTH
DAKOTA

WISCONSIN

IOWA

NEBRASKA

ILLINOIS

COLORADO

KANSAS

MISSOURI

OKLAHOMA

TENNESSEE

TEXAS

ARKANSAS

ALABAMA

11

They did not use a car when
they traveled. There were
no cars then. They rode in
a covered wagon.

The family settled in South Dakota. Laura began working as a teacher.

While she was living in South Dakota, Laura met a man named Almanzo Wilder. She and Almanzo married in 1885.

The Wilders had a daughter.
They named her Rose.

Rose grew up and became
a writer.

One day Rose had an idea.
She asked her mother to write
stories about her childhood.
Rose thought other people
would enjoy her mother's stories.

Laura sat down at her desk
and began to write.

LAURA INGALLS WILDER

# Little House
# in the Big Woods

ILLUSTRATED BY GARTH WILLIAMS

She wrote a book called
*Little House in the Big Woods*.
Children all over the world
loved it. They asked her to
write more.

Laura Ingalls Wilder wrote seven more books. They were called the "Little House" books. Suddenly, Laura was famous!

Laura did not let being famous change her life. She still worked on her farm every day. She thought hard work was good for a person.

Laura Ingalls Wilder lived to be 90 years old. She died on February 10, 1957.

Children are still reading Laura Ingalls Wilder's books.

There was even a television show based on them. It was called *Little House on the Prairie*. The show was very popular.

# Words You Know

Laura Ingalls Wilder

Almanzo Wilder

Rose Wilder

covered wagon

farm

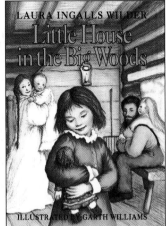

Little House in the
Big Woods

famous

# Index

# About the Author

More than fifty published books bear Wil Mara's name. He has written both fiction and nonfiction, for both children and adults. He lives with his family in northern New Jersey.

# Photo Credits

Photographs © 2003: Corbis Images: cover, 14 (Bettmann), 13 (David Muench), 3, 7, 31 top left; Ellen B. Senisi: 29; HarperCollins Publishers/Garth Williams: 22, 31 top right; Laura Ingalls Wilder Home Association, Mansfield, MO: 4, 8, 17, 18, 19, 21, 25, 26, 30 top left, 30 top right, 31 bottom; Les Kelly Publications/Leslie A. Kelly: 5.